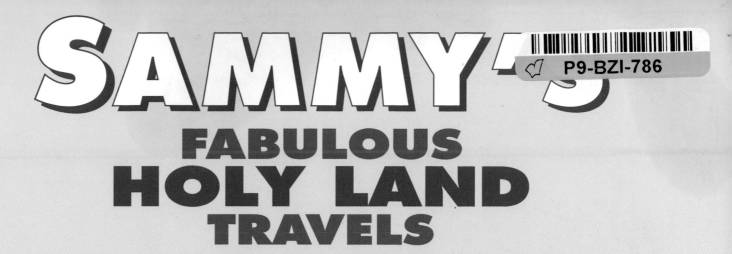

SAMMY'S
FABULOUS
HOLY LAND
TRAVELS

It all started because . . .

I am a shepherd boy. My days and nights are spent roaming the hills, caring for my sheep. It is a lonely life. I miss having friends to talk with.

One of the lambs, Sammy, usually stays close by my side. Sammy and I have become good friends. I enjoy talking to Sammy. I know that a sheep cannot really understand what I am telling him, but Sammy listens so closely, he almost seems to.

Lately I have been telling Sammy about the land of the Bible. I enjoy telling him about the Old Testament places where exciting things happened to the Israelites. God did some wonderful miracles to help His people. Sammy has heard about Egypt and the Red Sea, all the animals on the ark, and the promised land of Canaan.

I have told Sammy

stories from the New Testament, too. Just the other day I told him about Bethany, where Jesus had some very dear friends, Mary, Martha, and Lazarus. We talked about Galilee and what happened on the Damascus Road. There are so many interesting stories in the Bible; I never run out of things to talk about.

Sammy listens so closely, I wonder if he is thinking about what it would have been like to be in those places, right in the middle of the action.

See if you can find Sammy and me and the funny things at the bottom of each page in the following pictures. If you find everything, check the list in the back of the book for more things to look for.

Illustrated by
Daniel J. Hochstatter

Find Sammy, the Shepherd, and as many of these things as you can.

 Hang In There

 Iguana Pie

 Batty Bat

 Leapfrog

MOUNT ARARAT

God was tired of all the bad things people were doing. No one listened to Him anymore. No one tried to please Him. That is, no one except Noah.

So God told Noah to build a big boat, called an ark. God brought two of every kind of animal on earth and made them go into the ark. Then Noah and his wife and his sons and their wives went into the ark too. God closed the door of the ark.

Soon it started raining outside. It rained for forty days and forty nights. The whole earth was covered with a big flood, but Noah and his family and all the animals were safe because the ark floated on top of the water. Finally the rain ended and the flood waters started to go down. Noah's ark came to rest on the top of Mount Ararat. Noah and his family came out of the ark. They were the only people left on the earth because they loved God.

Hang Time

Frozen Treat Friends

Find Sammy, the Shepherd, and as many of these things as you can.

 Book Break

 Leaving Town

 Pitcher of Mouse

 Sherlock Sheep

EGYPT

Jacob was Abraham's grandson. After Jacob became an adult, God gave him the name Israel.

When Israel was very old, there was a famine in the land where he lived. So he and his sons took their families to live in Egypt. Israel's son Joseph already lived there, and he had made sure that everyone in Egypt had plenty of food. As the years passed, the Israelites grew to be a large part of Egypt's population.

Then a new king came to power in Egypt. He did not know about Joseph and the good things he had done for the country. He was afraid of the Israelites because there were so many of them. He thought they might help his enemies if a war broke out. So he made them become slaves of the Egyptians. The Israelites had to work very hard. One of their jobs was to make all the bricks used for the buildings and walls in Egypt. They even built two whole cities for the king.

Cellular Slave

Thirsty Slave

Find Sammy, the Shepherd, and as many of these things as you can.

 Rocket Sheep

 Beard Bridge

 Fishy Food Chain

 In a Pinch

THE RED SEA

The Israelites had been slaves of the Egyptians for a long time. God sent Moses and Aaron to lead them to freedom. Moses had to convince the Egyptian Pharaoh to let the Israelites go. God helped by placing ten terrible plagues on the Egyptian people.

Finally Pharaoh said the Israelites could go. But soon he changed his mind, and he sent his army to chase them. The Israelites were on the shore of the Red Sea, and the Egyptians were close behind. God's people were trapped! But God saved them with a miracle. He parted the waters of the Red Sea, and the Israelites crossed on dry ground. When the Egyptians tried to follow, the waters crashed down on them, and they were all drowned.

Cheese Chariot

Watercolor Artist

Find Sammy, the Shepherd, and as many of these things as you can.

 Cherry Picker

 Fast Food

 Rocket Man

 Up, Up, and Away

MOUNT SINAI

Moses climbed to the top of Mount Sinai because God had a special message to give him. God wrote the Ten Commandments telling His people how to live. He engraved them in stone with His finger.

God's commandments:

1. God should be first in your life.
2. Worship only God, not any kind of idol.
3. Do not take God's name in vain.
4. Remember God's Sabbath.
5. Treat your parents with respect.
6. Do not murder.
7. Do not commit adultery.
8. Do not steal.
9. Do not lie.
10. Do not covet what other people have.

Wrong Place, Wrong Time

A Little off the Top

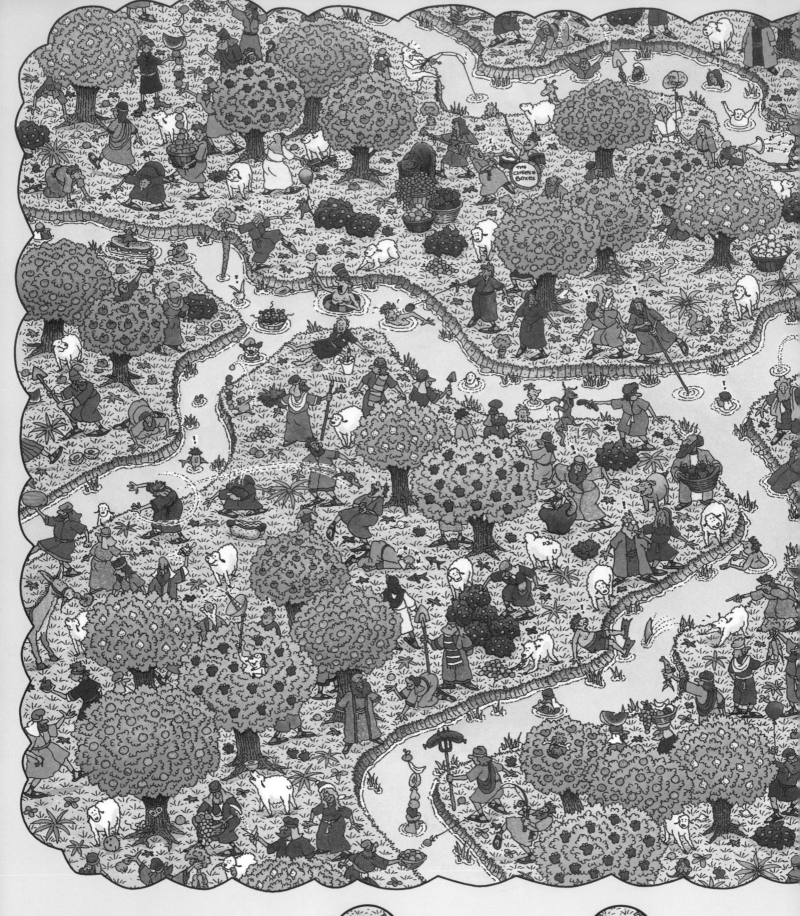

Find Sammy, the Shepherd, and as many of these things as you can.

 Hit It

 Sounds Fishy to Me

 Soggy Sub

 Wool Sweater

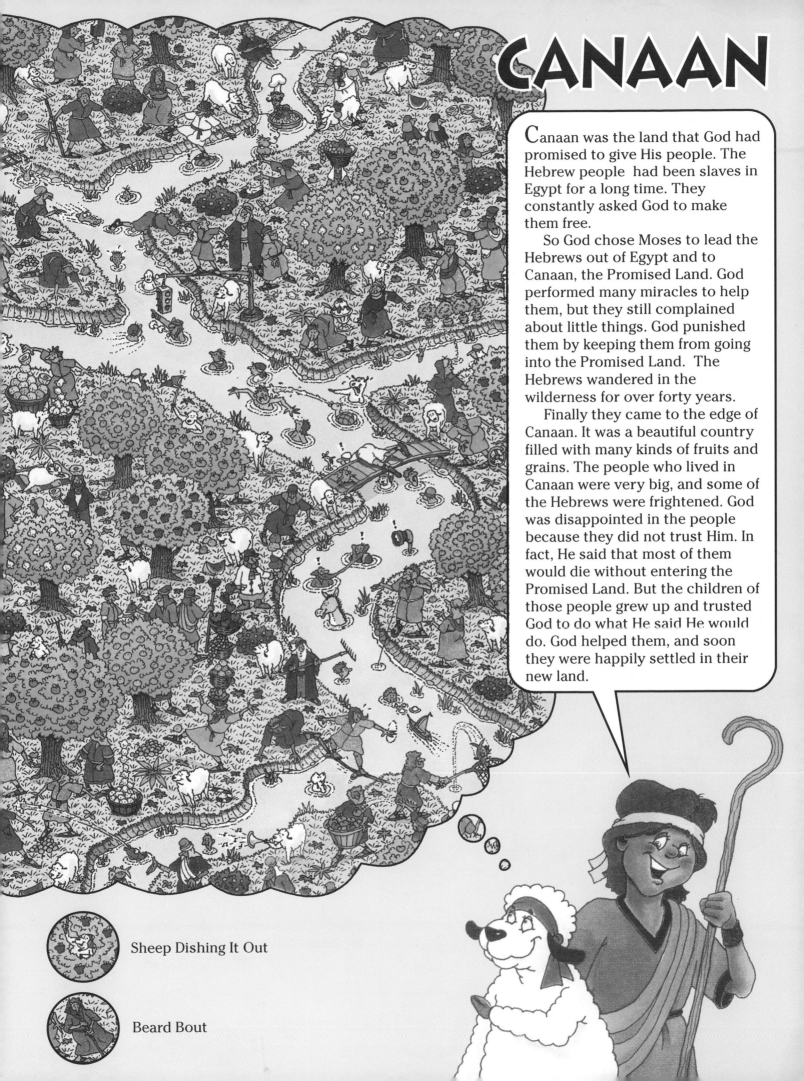

CANAAN

Canaan was the land that God had promised to give His people. The Hebrew people had been slaves in Egypt for a long time. They constantly asked God to make them free.

So God chose Moses to lead the Hebrews out of Egypt and to Canaan, the Promised Land. God performed many miracles to help them, but they still complained about little things. God punished them by keeping them from going into the Promised Land. The Hebrews wandered in the wilderness for over forty years.

Finally they came to the edge of Canaan. It was a beautiful country filled with many kinds of fruits and grains. The people who lived in Canaan were very big, and some of the Hebrews were frightened. God was disappointed in the people because they did not trust Him. In fact, He said that most of them would die without entering the Promised Land. But the children of those people grew up and trusted God to do what He said He would do. God helped them, and soon they were happily settled in their new land.

Sheep Dishing It Out

Beard Bout

Find Sammy, the Shepherd, and as many of these things as you can.

 Grape Wham

 Funny Bunny

 Radio Controlled

 Out of Lunch

NABOTH'S VINEYARD

Vineyards are fields where grapes are grown. In Bible times vineyards were very important because the grapes were used for food and to make wine.

A man named Naboth had a beautiful vineyard that had been in his family for years. He was proud of his vineyard. King Ahab decided he wanted to own Naboth's vineyard, but Naboth would not sell it to him. King Ahab's wife, Queen Jezebel, arranged for Naboth to be murdered so her husband could own the vineyard.

Ahab and Jezebel were not very nice people, and God punished them for the bad thing they did.

Doctor Concord

Woolback

Find Sammy, the Shepherd, and as many of these things as you can.

 Flutist

 Fresh Fish Sandwic[h]

 High Wire Wash

 Sharpshooter

NAZARETH

Nazareth was a small, unimportant village in Galilee. Some people said that nothing good could come out of Nazareth. But someone very special grew up there.

After Jesus was born in Bethlehem, an angel told Joseph to take his little family to Egypt. A bad king wanted to kill baby Jesus. When the bad king died, the angel said that Joseph, Mary, and Jesus could go home to Nazareth.

Jesus grew up there with His family. Joseph taught Him how to be a carpenter like he was. Jesus had chores to do, and He played with His friends. In some ways, Jesus seemed like any other boy, but He was very different. He was the Son of God.

Exterminator

Fore

Find Sammy, the Shepherd, and as many of these things as you can.

 Twin Mice

 Rodeo Rodent

 Pan Fish

 Sammy Seeker

THE WILDERNESS

A wilderness is a place where plants grow wild and not many people live. It may be a thick forest, or it may be a desert.

John the Baptist lived in the desert wilderness in Judea, not far from the Dead Sea. He wore clothes made from camel hair, and he ate locusts and wild honey.

John traveled around telling people that Jesus was coming. The message he gave helped the people get ready to hear what Jesus would tell them.

Photographer

Rocket Roller

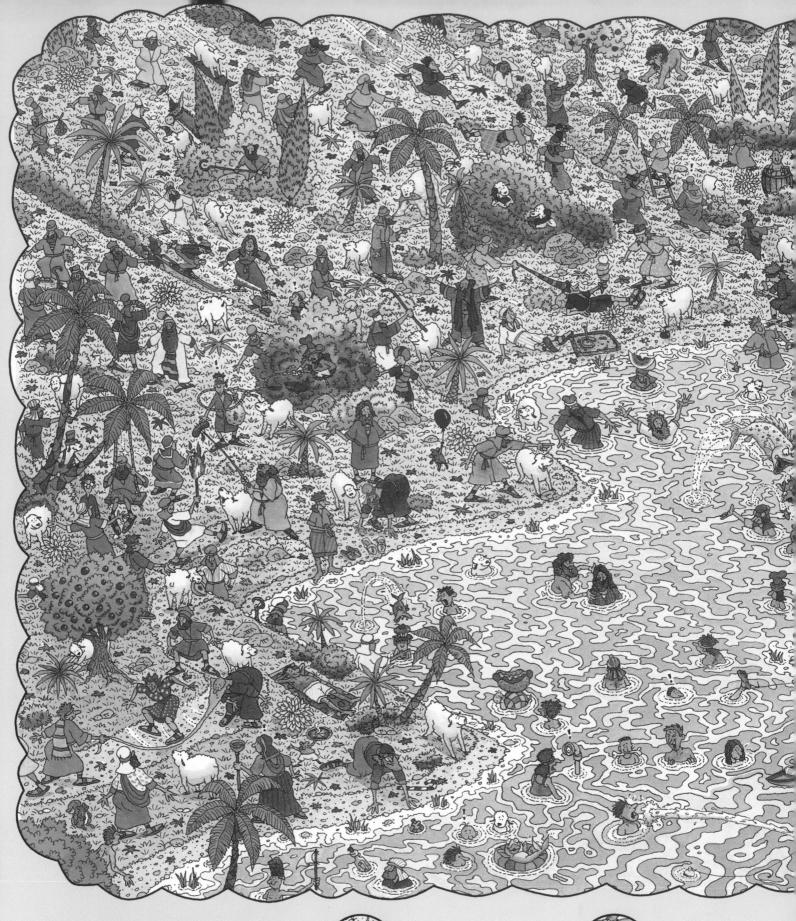

Find Sammy, the Shepherd, and as many of these things as you can.

 Party Animals

 Bob

 Suspendered Sheep

 Floating Fish

THE JORDAN RIVER

The Jordan River is the longest river in Palestine. Many important Bible events took place in or around the Jordan River.

John the Baptist was at the Jordan River teaching people about the Messiah who would come to save people from their sins. When a person believed in the Messiah, John baptized him in the Jordan River.

Jesus came and asked John to baptize Him. John knew this man was the Messiah and that Jesus should baptize him instead. But John did baptize Jesus because Jesus said that it was the right thing to do. Then God spoke from heaven saying, "This is My beloved Son, in whom I am well pleased."

Splitting Hairs

Horseshoe Headache

Find Sammy, the Shepherd, and as many of these things as you can.

 Roll for a Rodent

 Fast Fish

 Slingshot Sheep

 Foul Fish

GALILEE

One afternoon Jesus was teaching on a hillside in Galilee. More than five thousand people came out of the towns in the area to hear what He was teaching.

Jesus taught for many hours. The disciples said that He should send the people into the villages to eat dinner. But Jesus had a different idea. He wanted the disciples to feed the people. Of course, they did not have enough food to feed so many people. So Jesus took care of the problem.

Jesus asked if anyone in the crowd had food. One small boy had a lunch of five loaves of bread and two fish. Jesus took this small lunch, asked God's blessing, and fed all the people with it. The disciples even filled twelve baskets with what was left over! Everyone was amazed.

Three Men in a Tub

Cold Lamb

Find Sammy, the Shepherd, and as many of these things as you can.

 Ice Cream for Two

 Flower Girl

 Say What?

 Swiss Hotel

BETHANY

The small town of Bethany was the home of three of Jesus's special friends. Mary, Martha, and Lazarus—two sisters and a brother—played a big part in one of Jesus's most well-known miracles.

Lazarus was very sick, so his sisters sent for Jesus. They knew He could help their brother. But by the time Jesus arrived, Lazarus was dead.

Jesus knew that Mary, Martha, and Lazarus believed He was the Son of God. He went to the tomb of Lazarus and called for the dead man to come out. Lazarus walked out of the tomb, still wrapped in grave clothes. He was alive— and many people believed in Jesus that day!

Diver

Man with Paper Dolls

Find Sammy, the Shepherd, and as many of these things as you can.

 Fowl Play

 William I'm Telling

 Rat Roast

 Chilly Willy

JERUSALEM

Jerusalem was a large city where many people lived. In Jerusalem there were many businesses and a large church, called a temple.

People went to the temple to worship God. They usually brought animals to give as sacrifices to God. Some people had started selling animals in the temple for a lot of money. Jesus went to the temple to worship and saw these people cheating the poor. He did not like that. So Jesus chased them out of the temple. He told them that God's house was a place to worship, not a place to make money.

Column Climber

Southwestern Sheep

Find Sammy, the Shepherd, and as many of these things as you can.

 Angry Woman

 Mouse Juggler

 In the Spotlight

 Alien Mouse

THE DAMASCUS ROAD

Saul hated everyone who believed in Jesus. He tried to put Christians in jail and make them miserable in any way he could.

One day, Saul was on the Damascus Road. He had permission from the high priest to look for Christians in Damascus. Suddenly a bright light shone down on Saul, and he heard a voice. "Why are you persecuting Me, Saul?" the voice asked.

"Who are you?" Saul replied.

"I am Jesus, whom you are persecuting," the voice answered.

This convinced Saul that Jesus was really the Son of God and that He was alive. So Saul became a Christian. People started to call him Paul, and he spent the rest of his life telling people about Jesus. Paul wrote many books in the Bible.

Welder

Seed Shooter

Titles in
A Seeking Sammy Book
series:

Sammy's Fantastic Journeys
with the
Early Heroes of the Bible

Sammy's Incredible Travels
with
Jesus and His Friends

Sammy's Excellent
Real-Life Adventures

Sammy's Tree-Mendous
Christmas Adventure

Sammy's Fabulous
Holy Land Travels